COOKING SKILLS

PARTY FOOD

CLAUDIA MARTIN

E **Enslow Publishing**
101 W. 23rd Street
Suite 240
New York, NY 10011
USA

enslow.com

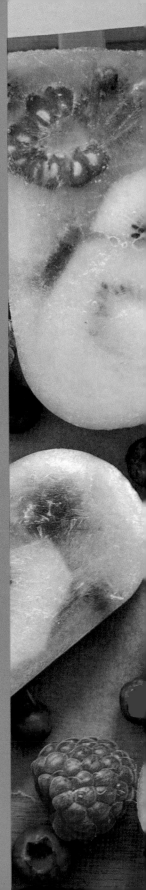

Published in 2019 by Enslow Publishing, LLC.
101 W. 23rd Street, Suite 240, New York, NY 10011

Copyright © 2019 Enslow Publishing, LLC

Editors: Sarah Eason and Jennifer Sanderson
Designers: Paul Myerscough and Simon Borrough
Picture Researcher: Claudia Martin

Cataloging-in-Publication Data
Names: Martin, Claudia.
Title: Party food / Claudia Martin.
Description: New York : Enslow Publishing, 2019. | Series: Cooking skills | Includes glossary and index.
Identifiers: ISBN 9781978506664 (pbk.) | ISBN 9781978506398 (library bound) | ISBN 9781978506336 (ebook)
Subjects: LCSH: Cooking—Juvenile literature. | Entertaining—Juvenile literature. | Parties—Juvenile literature. | Cookbooks—Juvenile literature.
Classification: LCC TX652.5 M35 2019 | DDC 641.5—dc23

Printed in the United States of America

To Our Readers: We have done our best to make sure all website addresses in this book were active and appropriate when we went to press. However, the author and the publisher have no control over and assume no liability for the material available on those websites or on any websites they may link to. Any comments or suggestions can be sent by e-mail to customerservice@enslow.com.

Photo Credits: Cover: Shutterstock: Dusan Zidar: tc; Monkey Business Images: bc; ommaphat chotirat: br; Rawpixel.com: bl. Inside: Shutterstock: Africa Studio: pp.20, 23t, 26–27, 39r, 41cr; Aleksandrs Samuilovs: p.38; Ariwasabi: pp.10–11; Armin Staudt: p.39l; Barbara Neveu: pp.34bc, 34br; Bartosz Luczak: pp.44–45; bitt24: p.21t; cobraphotography: pp.18–19; Deeanna Williams: p.24; Edith Frincu: p.12; Eliane Haykal: pp.12–13; Ezume Images: pp.20–21; Foxys Forest Manufacture: p.23b; fredredhat: p.36; gpointstudio: pp.4–5; Ileish Anna: pp.32–33; InnerVisionPRO: pp.28–29; its_al_dente: pp.1t, 11l; jabiru: p.27tc; Jaren Jai Wicklund: pp.40–41; javitrapero: p.44b; j.chizhe: p.11r; Joshua Resnick: p.15t; Kati Finell: p.29; Kseniia Perminova: p.34tr; Kseniya Bogdanova: p.17r; lenetstan: p.25l; LightField Studios: pp.27b, 31r; lightofchairat: p.44t; Liv friis-larsen: pp.42–43; Malykalexa: p.27tl; MaraZe: p.30; Matt Antonino: p.4; Michelle Lee Photography: p.27tr; Milles Studio: pp.8–9; Monkey Business Images: pp.1b, 9, 15b, 21b; Nataliia K: p.33c; NatashaPhoto: p.41cl; Oleksandra Naumenko: p.41bl; ommaphat chotirat: p.32; Pressmaster: p.43b; pumpuija: p.31l; Rawpixel.com: pp.6–7, 13b, 25r; Regreto: pp.30–31; Romrodphoto: pp.36–37; Shane White: p.19; Signe Leth: pp.2–3, 34–35, 46–47, 48; Swellphotography: p.33t; Teri Virbickis: p.18t; Tharakom: p.17l; Timolina: p.13t; Valentina_G: pp.14–15; View Apart: p.18b; vivooo: pp.24–25; wavebreakmedia: pp.22–23; XiXinXing: pp.16–17; Yakobchuk Viacheslav: p.37; zarzamora: pp.38–39; Zharinova Marina: pp.43t, 46.

CONTENTS

CHAPTER 1
GET COOKING!

Planning a party? Have you invited the whole block or is the party just for you and your best friend? Read on for delicious, easy-to-cook ideas that will make your party legendary.

Preparing a Feast

In this book, you will find a selection of recipes for popular party foods, from dependable dips to sweet treats. By preparing a range of these recipes, you can provide a buffet that gives everyone something to choose from, whatever their tastes or special diet. Cooking party food is always fun—but a bonus is that these recipes will also help you brush up your cooking skills and build a repertoire of new techniques, from making top tortillas to peeling tomatoes like a professional chef.

Planning a Menu

After you have decided on a guest list and sent out invitations, you need to plan your menu. Consider the number of guests and whether they have any dietary needs, intolerances, or allergies. You may need to label foods in a buffet ("meat," "eggs," or "wheat") and make sure you do not include any ingredients containing particular allergens, such as peanuts. Also consider the time of day of your party and whether your guests will be expecting to fill up or just nibble.

Does It Have to be Healthy?

The answer is probably no, since you are catering for a one-off treat. Yet it does no harm to remember that too much salt, sugar, and saturated fat (the "bad" fat, found in dairy products and meats, that can lead to heart disease) are not good for us. Also consider that, if you want your guests to feel satisfied after eating, you should include some carbohydrates, particularly whole grains such as those found in whole wheat tortillas. You should include some vegetables and fruits, as well as some low-fat protein and dairy.

Being Prepared

When you are planning a party, it is not just the food you need to think about. Here is a checklist of items you may need to buy, borrow, or find in the basement:

- Drinks
- Plates, cups, cutlery, and napkins
- Serving dishes and bowls
- Decorations
- Tables and chairs
- Music
- Cleaning supplies

READ THE RECIPE...

The countdown has started! Pick some recipes that will make your guests want to come back for more.

Choose a Range

If you want to provide food to please everyone, try picking recipes from across the whole book. If you want to serve some dips, turn to Chapter 2. To add some spice, flick to Chapter 3. To fill up everyone, look at Chapter 4 for a range of wrap ideas. For popcorn to pass around, try the delicious recipes in Chapter 5. If it is a pool party or barbecue, keep everyone cool with the popsicles in Chapter 6. Gooey desserts are very popular, so choose from the chocolate-dipped luxuries in Chapter 7.

How Much, How Hot?

In this book, measurements are given in ounces (oz), followed by grams (g), as well as cups, followed by milliliters (ml). There are 240 ml in each cup. Sometimes, you will be told to add a teaspoon (tsp) or tablespoon (tbsp) of an ingredient. There are 5 ml in a teaspoon and 15 ml in each tablespoon. When a "pinch" or a "sprinkle" is suggested, the exact amount is not so important—but take it easy if you are cooking with chili!

Oven temperatures are given in Fahrenheit (°F), followed by Celsius (°C). When cooking on a stove, if you do not know how hot to turn it, go for a low heat, then turn it up if the cooking is taking longer than the recipe suggests.

Go Shopping

When you have chosen your recipes, make a list of the ingredients and equipment you need. Consider the number of recipes you have chosen and the number of guests. Each recipe states the quantity of wraps or bowls of dip it makes. All the recipes are designed to be easy to multiply or divide, so you can make more wraps but less popcorn.

Start Cooking Early

When cooking for a party, it is better to prepare some food the night or morning before the party, then keep it in the refrigerator or in an airtight container as needed. Popsicles must be prepared and frozen eight hours in advance. Limit the number of foods, such as freshly fried quesadillas and warm chocolate sauce, that will keep your hands busy once your guests have arrived. When you start cooking, read the recipe instructions carefully. The ingredients are listed in the order they are used, which should help you not to forget anything. If you are nervous about your cooking skills, take a look at the "Mastering the Basics" sections at the start of each chapter.

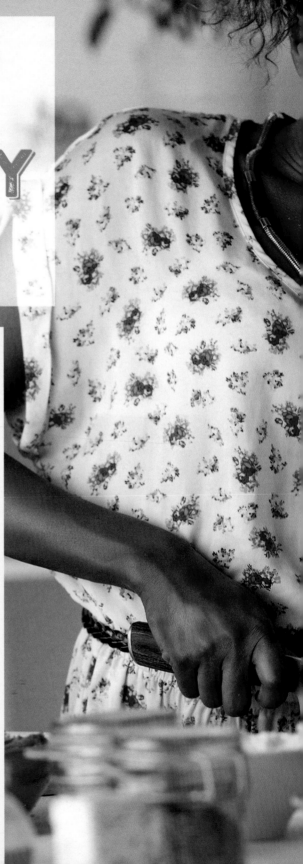

...OR GO YOUR OWN WAY

These recipes are just ideas to get your party started!

Test It Out

If there is time before your party, try out the recipes so you can iron out any glitches in advance. On this first try, you can play it safe by following the instructions closely and measuring the ingredients exactly. Then, when you taste the dish, ask yourself what you like about the flavors, textures, and presentation. Is the salsa too spicy? Do the wraps need more filling? Could the presentation be more colorful? The "Chef's Tip" box beside each recipe might offer ideas for adding different spices or flavorings. For even more ideas for ingredient changes and combinations, take a look at the "Switch It Up" boxes at the beginning of each chapter.

Special Diets

If you have invited vegetarian friends, all of the recipes are meat- and fish-free except the wraps on page 24. These can easily be made vegetarian friendly using the "Switch It Up" section for substitutions. To make the recipes vegan, you will need to remove—or switch in vegan alternatives for—eggs, cheese, milk, and other dairy products. If any of your friends has a gluten allergy, look out for tortillas that are labeled "gluten-free."

Keep It Clean

Hygiene is very important in any kitchen. Before cooking:
- Wash your hands with soap and warm water.
- Make sure all your work surfaces and equipment are clean.
- If you have long hair, tie it back.
- Wash produce under cold running water.
- Check the use-by dates on all ingredients.
- Do not leave fresh foods out of the refrigerator for more than two hours.
- Keep foods in an airtight container or covered in plastic wrap until serving.
- Do not reheat hot foods once they have cooled.

CHAPTER 2
DIPS

Dips are many people's favorite part of any party buffet. Just scoop them up with tortilla chips, carrot and cucumber sticks, crackers, or flatbreads.

Around the World

Dips are a fun way to offer world flavors at your party. Hummus (turn to page 12) is a Middle Eastern specialty. Guacamole (turn to page 14) was first made by the Aztecs in what is today Mexico. The name guacamole comes from the Aztec "ahuaca-mulli," which roughly translates as "avocado-mixture."

A Taste of Europe

Some other popular, easy-to-make dips have their origins in Europe. For example, tzatziki is a Greek specialty made from salted yogurt, cucumber, garlic, olive oil, lemon juice, and herbs. From southern France, there is olive tapenade, which is blended from finely chopped olives and olive oil. Tapenade is delicious on warm, crusty bread.

Mastering the Basics
Using a Food Processor or a Blender

The hummus recipe calls for using a food processor or hand-held blender. The benefit of this kind of gadget is that you can quickly process ingredients until they are smooth and fully combined. Here is how to use a food processor or blender safely:

1 If you are working with a hand-held blender, process the food inside a tall-sided bowl to avoid splashes. If using a food processor, put the ingredients in the jar before turning it on, then keep the lid on throughout use. Never put your fingers, spoons, or anything else in the bowl or jar while the appliance is on.

2 For extra safety, remove the jar from the base if you need to open the lid.

3 Leave hot ingredients to cool before processing, because steam can force off the lid or create a scalding splash.

4 Clean your appliance thoroughly after use. Put any removable, nonelectric parts in the dishwasher if possible. Bacteria can multiply easily in those hard-to-reach crevices.

Switch It Up

If you like the hummus recipe on page 12, try these colorful switches. Turn your hummus pink by adding 9 oz (255 g) of cooked beets to the blend. Or make herby hummus by adding ½ cup (15 g) chopped fresh parsley and ¼ cup (7 g) fresh tarragon to the mix.

HUMMUS

This recipe makes around two dipping bowls of this favorite Middle Eastern dip.

chickpeas

You Will Need
15 oz (425 g) can of chickpeas
3 garlic cloves
4 tbsp lemon juice
   (from around 2 lemons)
3 tsp ground cumin
2 tbsp tahini (sesame paste)
Pinch of salt
8 tbsp water
4 tbsp olive oil
Sprinkle of paprika to garnish

Instructions
1 Drain the chickpeas and reserve a few whole chickpeas to garnish.
2 Peel and slice your garlic cloves.
3 Put the chickpeas, lemon juice, garlic, cumin, tahini, and salt in a food processor (or use a hand-held blender). Blend until you have a stiff paste.
4 Add a little water, blend for a moment, then check your consistency. Continue until you have a smooth paste. Do not add so much water that your hummus will drip off a tortilla chip.
5 To serve, add the olive oil, a sprinkling of paprika, and some whole chickpeas.

Serve with sticks of carrot, celery, and cucumber.

CHEF'S TIP

If you do not have any cumin, increase the tahini by 1 tbsp for more flavor.

GUACAMOLE

Everyone loves a bowl of fresh and tangy guacamole to scoop up with a tortilla chip or vegetable stick.

You Will Need
3 medium avocados
1 medium tomato
1 small red onion
Handful of cilantro
1 lime
Salt and pepper

Instructions
1 Halve the avocados and remove the pits. Slicing slippery avocados often causes injuries: always cut away from your fingers and do not try to remove the pit with a knife. Using a spoon, scoop the flesh into a mixing bowl.
2 Chop the tomato into small pieces, then add to the bowl of avocados.
3 Peel, halve, and finely chop the onion—slice downward onto a cutting board, first one way and then the other, making crisscross cuts. Add the onion to the other ingredients.
4 Chop the cilantro leaves and stalks, then add to the bowl.
5 Cut the lime in half and squeeze it for its juice, then pour into the mix.
6 Mash your ingredients using a fork or potato masher.
7 Taste, then add a little salt and pepper as needed.
8 Serve immediately so your guacamole does not turn brown.

Your guests will keep coming back for more!

CHEF'S TIP

If you cannot serve right away, put an avocado pit into the bowl to slow the flesh browning, cover with plastic wrap, and refrigerate.

CHAPTER 3
SPICING IT UP

Spicy finger foods give a great burst of flavor, and will mark your party spread as a bit different from the usual sandwiches, chips, and peanuts displays.

Chili Cheats

Both the recipes in this chapter are Mexican-style dishes that have been spiced up with chili peppers. Nervous about cooking with chilis in case your guests have to go running for the drinks table? Just choose your chilis wisely. The color of a chili is no marker of its strength: all chilis ripen from green to orange to red. Small chilis are usually hotter than large ones. To cut back on the heat, remove a chili's seeds and inner veins.

Other Ideas

For ideas for other exciting finger foods, turn to Asian-style recipes. How about creating your own take on spring rolls by buying ready-made rice pancakes, then filling with your choice of stir-fried vegetables, ginger, garlic, and chili flakes? Serve with a soy dipping sauce.

Switch It Up

If you enjoy cooking with chili, how about making spicy garlic bread? You will need a split-open baguette, spread with a mix of 2 oz (55 g) softened butter, 4 peeled and crushed garlic cloves, 3 tbsp chopped parsley, and 2 tsp dried chili flakes. Wrap in foil and bake in the oven at 360°F (180°C) for about ten minutes.

Mastering the Basics:
Peeling Tomatoes

The salsa recipe on page 18 calls for peeled tomatoes. That is because, when tomato skin finds its way into dishes, it forms little chewy curls. Learning how to peel tomatoes is a useful skill. Here is how to do it:

1 Wash the tomatoes, then cut away the stem. Cut a shallow cross on the bottom of each tomato—this will make peeling them easier.
2 Fill a large saucepan with water and bring it to a boil. Using a spoon, carefully slide in the tomatoes.
3 Leave the tomatoes in the boiling water for thirty seconds, while you fill a large bowl with icy water.
4 Drain the tomatoes into a colander, then put them in the icy water.
5 After five minutes, the tomato skins should be curling away from the flesh.
6 Using your fingers, simply peel away the skin.

TOMATO SALSA

This makes 2 cups (480 ml) of the classic dip for tortilla chips—or use it to spice up burritos, tacos, or anything else.

jalapeños

Fresh, tasty—and with a kick of chili!

You Will Need
½ small white onion, peeled
2 garlic cloves
18 oz (520 g) tomatoes
1 or 2 chili peppers, depending
   on taste
Small handful of cilantro
1 lime
Salt and pepper

Instructions
1 Finely chop the onion.
2 Peel the garlic cloves. Slice them thinly, then cut the slices into small pieces.
3 Peel the tomatoes (see page 17), halve them, scoop out and discard the seeds, then chop the flesh into small chunks.
4 Cut the stems from the chilis, then halve them lengthways. Using the tip of a knife, carefully scrape away the seeds and veins. Chop the flesh into small pieces. When preparing chilis, never touch your eyes with your fingers. Wash your hands thoroughly.
5 Chop the cilantro leaves and stems.
6 Halve the lime, then squeeze it for its juice.
7 In a mixing bowl, stir the onion, garlic, tomatoes, chilis, cilantro, and lime juice together. Add salt and pepper to taste.
8 To give the flavor time to mature, refrigerate for at least two hours before serving.

CHEF'S TIP

For a milder chili taste, use banana or Cubanelle chilis. For more heat, use jalapeño or New Mexican green.

BAKED NACHOS

Depending on how hungry your guests are feeling, this recipe will serve around eight people.

You Will Need

10 oz (285 g) bag of plain tortilla chips
8 oz (225 g) cheese, grated
15 oz (425 g) can black beans
1 small red onion, peeled and finely chopped
Handful of black olives
1 or 2 green chilis, depending on taste, chopped
½ cup (120 ml) salsa (see recipe on page 18)
4 tbsp sour cream
1 medium avocado, peeled and chopped
2 large tomatoes, chopped

Instructions

1 Preheat the oven to 370°F (190°C).
2 Cover two baking sheets with aluminum foil. Place the tortilla chips on the covered sheets.
3 Sprinkle over the cheese, black beans, onion, olives, and chilis.
4 Bake in the oven for twelve minutes, or until the cheese has melted and the tortilla chips are heated through.
5 Slide your nachos onto serving plates, then garnish with the salsa, sour cream, avocado, and tomatoes.

black olives

Cooked in a moment
and eaten in a flash!

CHEF'S TIP

For even more of a wow
factor, swap the chopped
avocado for some guacamole
(see recipe on page 14).

CHAPTER 4
WRAPS

Wraps are a perfect party food because they are easy for your guests to hold as they chat and wander. They are also simple to prepare a few hours in advance, leaving you free to enjoy your party.

Tortilla Time

Tortillas are thin Central American flatbreads made from ground white, yellow, and blue corn. They can also be made from wheat flour. Tortillas are perfect for making wraps because they are strong enough to hold your filling. They can be used for roll-ups (see page 24), folded and fried quesadillas (see page 26), and burritos, which are rolled and then folded at the bottom for security.

Farther Afield

Tortillas are not your only choice for wraps. For a lighter and more Asian taste and texture, try rice pancakes. For a low-carb vegetarian dish, use lettuce or Swiss chard leaves. Other flatbreads perfect for wraps include Armenian lavash, which can be filled with kebab meat for a traditional Turkish dürüm wrap, and Middle Eastern pita, which could be filled with meat and tzatziki to make a Greek gyro.

dough

Mastering the Basics
Tortillas

You can buy different types of tortilla in a store, but there is nothing better than homemade tortillas! Here is how to make eight of them:

1 Put 2 cups (240 g) all-purpose flour in a large bowl along with ½ tsp salt. Stir in ¾ cup (180 ml) water and 3 tbsp olive oil.

2 Put your dough on a clean surface dusted with flour. Knead the dough by using the base of your hand to squash and push it away from you, stretching it a little. Put the dough back into a ball, give it a quarter turn, and repeat around nine more times.

3 Cover your dough with an upturned bowl and let it rest for ten minutes.

4 Divide the dough into eight equal portions. On the same lightly floured surface, use a rolling pin to roll each portion into a circle roughly 7 inches (18 cm) across.

5 Heat a little oil in a non-stick skillet or frying pan, then fry each tortilla for one minute on each side, until lightly browned.

Switch It Up

If you like the style of the roll-ups on page 24, how about switching your fillings? For vegetarian friends, try carrot and hummus, using about 1 grated medium carrot and 3 tbsp hummus per tortilla. For a meatier wrap, use three thin slices of cooked chicken, 1 tbsp grated cheese, 1 finely chopped small tomato, and 2 tbsp hummus per tortilla.

SALMON ROLLS

Impress your friends with these delicious rolls and their fancy-sounding name—rotolos.

chives

Beautiful to look at, simple to make.

You Will Need

10 oz (285 g) cream cheese
1 tbsp lemon juice
2 tbsp chopped chives
2 lettuce leaves (finely chopped)
Black pepper
4 flour tortillas
12 oz (340 g) smoked salmon

Instructions

1. In a bowl, mix together the cream cheese, lemon juice, chives, and lettuce. Season with pepper.
2. Spread the cream cheese mixture over the tortillas. Cover with the smoked salmon.
3. Roll up the tortillas like a spiral. Cut off the untidy ends.
4. Wrap each roll tightly in plastic wrap, then chill in the refrigerator for at least two hours.
5. When you are ready to serve, slice each roll into evenly sized, easy-to-hold pieces.

CHEF'S TIP

For a cooler, slightly aniseedy flavor, swap the chives for fresh dill.

PUMPKIN QUESADILLAS

Forget the pumpkin pie—these pumpkin treats are anything but old-fashioned!

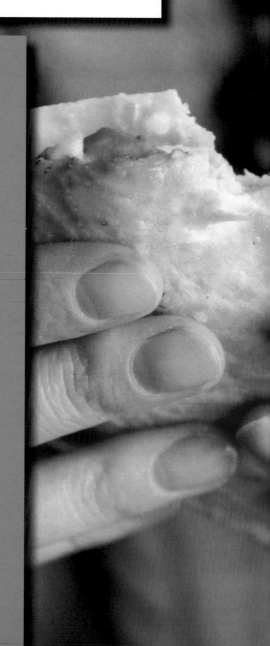

You Will Need
15 oz (425 g) can of pumpkin puree
2 tsp ground cumin
8 flour tortillas
4 oz (115 g) goat's cheese, crumbled
2–4 tbsp vegetable oil

Instructions
1 In a bowl, mix together the pumpkin puree and cumin.
2 Spread the pumpkin mixture over half of each tortilla, then sprinkle over the crumbled cheese.
3 Fold each tortilla in half. Press down lightly to stick together.
4 Heat 1 tbsp oil in a frying pan. Place one folded tortilla in the pan, then fry over a medium heat for one to two minutes. Slide a spatula under the open side, then flip the quesadilla over on the fold. Fry for one to two minutes on the other side. Repeat with the other tortillas, adding a little extra oil each time.
5 When the tortillas have cooled a little, slice each one in half.

goat's cheese

cumin

Gooey, cheesy, and satisfying!

CHEF'S TIP

This recipe makes sixteen quesadilla wedges. Too many? Too few? Just halve or double the recipe!

CHAPTER 5

POPCORN

Popcorn is fun to eat and easily flavored to be salty, sweet, sticky, or spicy. With a little ingenuity, you can even color it every shade of the rainbow.

Look a Little Closer

We are so used to eating popcorn that most of us probably never wonder what exactly we are eating. Popcorn is made from a special variety of corn kernel, or seed, that pops and expands—to many times its original size—when heated. People have been eating popcorn for thousands of years—remnants of 5,600-year-old popcorn have been found in what is now Mexico.

Naughty or Nice

Air-popped popcorn is packed with fiber and contains no sugar or salt, so on its own, popcorn is very good for you. However, when we pop corn in rich oils like coconut, then slather it in sugar or salt, it becomes a lot less healthy. This means this type of popcorn is perfect for a party treat but not ideal for everyday snacking.

Switch It Up

To make chocolate popcorn, spread out about 8 cups (90 g) popped corn over parchment-covered baking sheets then drizzle with 4 oz (115 g) melted chocolate (see page 41). Set in the refrigerator for ten minutes. To make colored popcorn, boil 1 cup (225 g) sugar, ½ tbsp butter, 4 tbsp water, and a few drops of food coloring for three minutes. Cool for ten minutes, then gently stir through 8 cups (90 g) popped corn. Leave to dry on parchment paper.

Mastering the Basics
Popping Corn

If you own a popcorn maker, it is really easy to pop corn—but making perfect popcorn on the stovetop is a more delicate skill. You want to get all the kernels to burst, but not stick to the bottom of the pan. Here is how to make one large bowlful, or about 8 cups:

1 Use a large, thick-bottomed pan with a lid.
2 Add about 3 tbsp coconut or canola oil, which are oils that will not get smoky unless they really overheat.
3 Heat the pan over a medium heat. You need to test when the oil is hot enough, so add a couple of kernels, put on the lid, and wait for them to pop.
4 As soon as you hear the kernels pop, pour about ⅓ cup (50 g) of kernels into the pan. Never put more than about ½ cup (80 g) of kernels in one pan since they need room to expand.
5 Put on the lid, leaving it open just a tiny crack to release steam and prevent the popcorn from becoming soggy.
6 Shake the pan every ten seconds to shift the kernels around.
7 Wait for the popping to stop or to slow to once every few seconds.

CARAMEL POPCORN

This luxurious popped corn puts the popcorn you buy at the movie theater to shame.

brown sugar

You Will Need

8 cups (90 g) popped corn (see the recipe on page 29)
5 oz (140 g) unsalted butter
6 oz (170 g) brown sugar
¼ tsp baking soda
¼ tsp salt

Instructions

1 Preheat the oven to 250°F (120°C). Cover two large baking sheets with aluminum foil.
2 In a saucepan, melt the butter over medium heat, then stir in the sugar.
3 Turn up the heat, bringing the mixture to a boil. Continue boiling for three to four minutes, stirring continuously to make sure the mixture does not stick to the bottom of the saucepan.
4 Remove the pan from the heat, then add the baking soda and salt. The sauce will bubble up, but keep stirring until it is thickened.
5 Pour the caramel sauce over the popcorn and stir to coat, then spread the corn evenly over the baking sheets.
6 Bake in the oven for one hour, stirring every fifteen to twenty minutes to break up clumps of corn.
7 Leave to cool before serving.

Caramel and popcorn make a fantastic combination.

CHEF'S TIP

For a richer flavor, add 1 tsp of vanilla essence to the caramel sauce in step 4.

LEMON AND ROSEMARY POPCORN

You can feel (a little bit) virtuous if you serve this popcorn because there is no sugar in sight.

Fresh, light, and zingy!

lemon zest

rosemary

You Will Need

½ a lemon
1 sprig of fresh rosemary
2 oz (55 g) unsalted butter
8 cups (90 g) popped corn
   (see the recipe on page 29)
Salt

Instructions

1 Collect the zest (outer peel) from the half lemon by lightly grating it. Then squeeze the lemon for about 1 tbsp of its juice.
2 Pick the leaves from the rosemary stem and chop them finely.
3 In a small saucepan, melt the butter over a low heat, then add the lemon zest and rosemary.
4 Stir for a few moments, without letting the butter brown.
5 Remove from the heat and stir in the lemon juice.
6 Pour the sauce over the popcorn, mix thoroughly, and add salt to taste.

CHEF'S TIP

If you cannot find fresh rosemary, use about ⅓ tsp of the dried herb.

CHAPTER 6
ICE POPS

Homemade popsicles are a perfect choice for summer parties, pool parties, and barbecues. All you need is a freezer, some molds, and a little know-how.

Collect Equipment

Popsicle molds are sold in larger supermarkets and hardware stores as well as online. Molds come in many shapes, from ordinary cylinders to hearts and bunnies. Flexible silicone molds make it easier to pull out your pops and are also simpler to clean. You could make your own molds from plastic cups, with a wooden popsicle stick pressed into position while freezing—find the right moment, when the popsicle is just firm enough to hold the stick in place.

Pick Your Ingredients

Fruit juices or blended fruit are good bases for popsicles. For a creamier taste, use yogurt or a mixture of cream, milk, or condensed milk. Adding pieces of whole fruit, such as berries, oranges, kiwis, mangoes, and pineapple, looks pretty and adds texture. Once the pops are frozen, you could gently dip them in cooled, melted chocolate (see page 41) and sprinkles, then return to the freezer.

Mastering the Basics
Making Popsicles

Once you know how to make popsicles, they are really easy party treats. Here is how to do it:

1 Use dry molds that have been freshly washed in hot soapy water.

2 Take extra care with the usual hygiene rules when making any food that will be frozen.

3 When pouring in your ingredients, leave a little room at the top of your molds, since the pops will expand as they freeze.

4 Depending on your ingredients, your pops will take four to eight hours to freeze.

5 To release the frozen pops from their molds, warm them under warm water or with your hands.

6 For the best flavor and texture, homemade pops are best eaten within a week, but they will keep in the freezer for up to two months.

7 Never refreeze partially defrosted pops, because bacteria will have multiplied in the pops as they thawed.

Switch It Up

Making a straightforward popsicle is simple, but how about something fancier? To create layered pops, first prepare the ingredients for all your layers. Pour the first layer into the bottom of the mold, while the other layers chill in the refrigerator. After two hours in the freezer, the bottom layer will be firm enough for you to pour on the second layer. Then return to the freezer for another two hours, and so on.

STRAWBERRY MILK POPS

This recipe makes twelve amazing popsicles for your pool party!

You Will Need
14 oz (400 g) strawberries
1 cup (240 ml) milk
14 oz (400 g) can condensed milk

Instructions
1. Wash the strawberries, then hull them to remove the leafy top and hard core (called the "calyx"). You can do this with a small but sharp-tipped knife, cutting in a circular motion around the leaves and a little way into the flesh beneath.
2. Blend the strawberries in a food processor until smooth.
3. Mix in the fresh milk and condensed milk.
4. Pour into twelve popsicle molds, then freeze for six to eight hours.

Ice cold and well worth the wait!

CHEF'S TIP

For a healthier option, use low-fat milk and "light" condensed milk.

ORANGE AND CARROT POPS

How about serving twelve of these sunshine-colored healthy treats?

You Will Need
10 medium carrots, peeled
6 oranges, cut in half

Instructions
1 You need to collect the juice from the carrots. If you have a juicer, this is simple. If not, grate the carrots and place in a muslin cloth. Put a large bowl underneath, then gather up the edges of the cloth, squeezing to press the carrot juice into the bowl. Another option is to press the grated carrot through a strainer. When you have as much juice as possible, discard the pulp.
2 Squeeze the juice from the oranges.
3 Lightly grate the skin of a couple of the oranges to collect the zest (outer peel).
4 In a large measuring cup, mix together the carrot juice and the orange juice and zest. If necessary, add cold water to make 3 cups (720 ml).
5 Pour into twelve molds, then freeze for six to eight hours.

Cool down with one of these popsicles.

CHEF'S TIP

No time to grate and juice?
Use about 2 cups (480 ml) of
store-bought orange juice and
1 cup (240 ml) of carrot juice.

CHAPTER 7

DIPPED IN CHOCOLATE

Serving foods that are dipped in chocolate looks luxurious and tastes delicious.

Chocolate Fondue

When melted chocolate is presented for dipping while still liquid, it is called a fondue. To keep the sauce fluid, each cup of melted chocolate is often mixed with about ¼ cup (60 ml) milk or cream, along with a little melted butter. The sauce needs to be made shortly before serving, or made in advance and rewarmed. Popular picks to dip in the fondue include marshmallows, crackers, wafers, meringues, and fruit.

Fondue can be messy, so make sure you provide skewers, forks, plates, and napkins.

Dipped and Cooled

A less messy but no less tasty option is to dip foods in chocolate, then leave the coating to set firm in the refrigerator. A favorite choice for this style of dipping is strawberries (see page 42), but switching in other fruits, such as apples, cherries, or citrus segments, also works well. Another fun and simple option is to dip store-bought cookies—making them look homemade!

Mastering the Basics
Melting Chocolate

When dipping in melted chocolate or baking with chocolate, knowing how to melt it is an essential skill. You cannot melt chocolate over direct heat—it will burn or lose its smooth texture. Here is how to do it:

1 You will need a heatproof bowl that fits over the top of a small saucepan—not so small that it gets jammed in tightly and not so big that it will fall off.

2 Break the chocolate into small pieces and place it in the heatproof bowl.

3 Put 1 to 2 inches (2.5–5 cm) of cold water in the saucepan. Make sure the water does not touch the bottom of the bowl. Bring the water to a boil, then reduce to a gentle simmer.

4 Place the heatproof bowl with your chocolate over the saucepan and allow the steam to melt the chocolate. Stir occasionally until melted, which should take two to three minutes.

5 Use oven mitts when removing the bowl, because the steam will be scalding hot.

Switch It Up

To make chocolate-dipped apple wedges, follow the recipe on page 42, switching in five apples. Core each apple and cut into eight wedges. To slow the apple browning, soak the wedges in a medium-sized bowl of water, containing ¼ cup (60 ml) lemon juice. Pat dry before dipping in chocolate and sprinkling with chopped walnuts or grated coconut. Serve within one to two hours.

CHOCOLATE STRAWBERRIES

Your guests will feel really spoiled when you bring out these gorgeous treats.

You Will Need
40 medium strawberries
8 oz (225 g) of semisweet or
   bittersweet chocolate

Instructions
1 Melt the chocolate according to the instructions on page 41.
2 While the chocolate melts, wash the strawberries thoroughly. Do not remove the leaves.
3 Place parchment paper or aluminum foil on a couple of trays large enough for your strawberries to be laid out without touching.
4 Holding each strawberry by the leaves, swirl it in the chocolate to coat, then place on the parchment or foil.
5 Refrigerate for thirty minutes until the chocolate is firm. Keep refrigerated until nearly ready to serve, particularly in hot weather.

A luxurious way to serve fruit!

CHEF'S TIP

For more variety in taste and presentation, dip half your strawberries in 4 oz (115 g) of melted white chocolate chips.

CHURROS

These traditional Spanish pastries are served with a chocolate dipping sauce.

You Will Need
4 oz (115 g) butter
1 cup (240 ml) water
1 cup (125 g) all-purpose flour
3 eggs
1 tsp vanilla extract
5 tbsp super-fine sugar
2 tsp ground cinnamon
2 cups (480 ml) melted chocolate (see page 41)

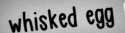
whisked egg

Instructions
1 Preheat the oven to 360°F (180°C).
2 Put the butter and water in a saucepan and bring to a boil.
3 Remove the saucepan from the heat and stir in the flour.
4 In a bowl, whisk together the eggs and vanilla extract.
5 Whisk the egg mixture into the ingredients in the saucepan a little at a time. Using an electric whisk will be quicker and easier, if you have one.
6 Spoon the mixture into a piping bag with a large star-shaped nozzle. If you do not have one, use a freezer bag with a 0.5-inch (1.25 cm) hole cut in the corner.
7 On a baking sheet covered with parchment paper, pipe your mixture into 4-inch (10-cm) lines, leaving 1 inch (2.5 cm) between the lines.
8 Bake for about twenty minutes until golden.
9 Combine the super-fine sugar and cinnamon, then sprinkle it over the hot churros.
10 Serve while still warm, with melted chocolate for dipping.

Crispy on the outside and soft on the inside!

CHEF'S TIP

If your mixture starts to get too runny in step 5 (it should be fairly thick, like mashed potato), leave out a little of your egg.

GLOSSARY

bake To cook food in an oven without liquid or fat.

boil When a liquid is so hot that it releases large bubbles of gas.

carbohydrates Food molecules contained in starchy foods, such as pasta, grains, and potatoes, as well as sugars and fibers, which provide most of your energy.

chili The small, hot-tasting seed case from particular types of pepper plant.

cilantro The green leaves of the coriander plant.

cinnamon A spice made from the bark of a Southeast Asian tree.

dill An herb with feathery leaves and a slightly bitter taste.

fiber Long molecules that are contained in plants and help with digestion.

fondue A dish in which pieces of food are dipped into a hot sauce, often made from chocolate or cheese.

fry To cook in hot oil or fat.

garlic clove One of the sections of a bulb of garlic.

gluten A mixture of two proteins found in cereal grains such as wheat, barley, rye, and some oats.

gyro A Greek dish made of meat cooked on a vertical rotisserie, usually served wrapped in a flatbread such as pita, with tomato, onion, and tzatziki.

intolerances Inabilities to eat a food without having side effects.

knead To massage and squeeze dough with the hands.

protein A substance found in lentils, beans, nuts, seeds, meat, fish, eggs, and dairy products that is essential for growth and health.

quesadillas Tortillas folded over a cheesy filling then fried.

saturated fat A type of "unhealthy" fat that is usually found in animal products such as meat and dairy.

simmer Heat enough to bubble gently but not to boil.

tzatziki A Greek side dish made from yogurt, cucumber, and garlic.

vegan A person who does not eat any animal products, including eggs, milk products, and honey.

whisk To stir, or beat, ingredients using the quick movement of a wire utensil, with the aim of introducing air to the mixture.

whole grains Grains obtained from cereal crops, such as wheat, that have not had their nutritious germ (kernel) and bran (outer layer) removed.

FURTHER READING

Books:

Bolte, Mari. *Awesome Recipes You Can Make and Share.*
North Mankato, MN: Snap Books, 2015.

Cerone, Lulu. *PhilanthroParties: A Party Planning Guide for Kids Who Want to Give Back.* New York, NY: Aladdin, 2017.

Federman, Carolyn. *New Favorites for New Cooks.* Berkeley, CA:
Ten Speed Press, 2018.

Owen, Ruth. *I Can Throw a Party!* New York, NY: Windmill Books, 2018.

Websites:

Cooking Tips and Resources
kidshealth.org/en/teens/whats-cooking.html
Discover more cooking tips here.

Serving Up Safe Buffets
www.fda.gov/Food/ResourcesForYou/Consumers/ucm328131.htm
Get advice on keeping your party food bacteria-free.

Teen Birthday Party Planner
www.thespruce.com/teen-birthday-party-planner-2610503
Read advice on planning parties for parents and teens.

28 Essential Party Snacks
www.geniuskitchen.com/ideas/best-party-snacks-6066
Find recipes and ideas for party snacks.

INDEX